Welcoming

Spring

E. Lee Vought

To order additional copies of this book, contact:
Xlibris
844-714-8691
www.Xlibris.com
Orders@Xlibris.com

Book Designer: s . a . m .

ISBN: 978-1-4257-6378-7 (sc)
ISBN: 978-1-4257-8493-5 (hc)

Library of Congress Control Number: 2007901539

Print information available on the last page

Rev. date: 02/08/2023

THE BEGINNING:

Many years ago, my friend, Eva, who lived in the same apartment building I did, told me she was going to silk-screen some note cards. I told her I'd be interested in learning how to do silk-screening and we set up a time to meet in her apartment. When I arrived, she said I needed to create a stencil out of paper. It was nearing the winter holidays, but, I couldn't think of anything to make into a stencil except the cut snowflakes we made when we were children. So a snowflake it was. It was messy — but fun. I liked the simplicity of the art form. For the most part, you have to stick with your design, good or bad. In oil painting, I always reworked, and reworked, and reworked. Well, you get the idea.

A few years later, when Kimber and I were living at the beach in Delaware, we had a room we called "the studio" and I was determined to do more artwork. The "studio" had served the prior owner as an architect's office and there was an architectural table built into the wall of that room and cabinets built into the barn wood walls to store supplies.

So, with Christmas approaching, I wanted to silk-screen the holiday cards. Unfortunately, I got busy, and the holiday slipped by — un-celebrated by hand-made greeting cards. I thought New Year cards would be novel. Again, that holiday passed by and again I failed to carry out my artistic plan. I said, "Oh, well, there is always next year." Kimber countered with, "Why not Spring Cards? We like Spring and its renewal and nobody sends Spring Cards."

The first Spring Card did not go smoothly – to say the least. I had trouble getting the necessary paints and other supplies. (In those days, I used to joke that you had to drive 45 minutes north or south just to get pantyhose – especially in the winter. All those "open year round" shops did not include November through March!!)

I then decided that I would make a woodcut for our Spring Card. The idea for "Sailing Into Spring" had been a pleasant dream – a sailboat with lots of daffodils in the foreground. The nightmare that followed included a trip to the Doctor's office after I dug the cutting tool into my hand that necessitated a tetanus shot. Needless to say, I returned to the safer art of silk-screening, especially after I realized I had applied the design incorrectly to the wood block and the design would print reverse of how I intended!! I telephoned an art supply store in Philadelphia where I had purchased my first silk-screen kit and ordered the paints I would need for the project. The first year we sent about 100 cards to friends and family. The reaction was wonderful — calls, letters, and notes from people who were surprised and elated at receiving the Springtime message.

Our tradition was born:

1977

SAILING INTO SPRING

"We wish you smooth sailing into Spring!"

1978

SPRING GARDEN

"A Spring Garden to wish you Happy Spring"

    With this card I envisioned a shower of colorful spring flowers – including my favorites. Again, we printed the daffodil and also tulips, with blue to present a trio of primary colors. With silk-screening, a separate screen is needed for each color – so it took 3 days, instead of one, to produce this card, because each color should dry, usually overnight, before the next color is applied.

    It was at this early juncture, I decided that I needed to keep the card simple and stick to one or two colors at most. I never looked for perfection, just a good design and an uplifting message. Kimber was usually in charge of the message, but there are exceptions as you will see.

1979

DOGWOOD

"Our very best Springtime Greetings!"

This card is one of my favorites. I think it is a good design and the register (how the two screens line up) is good.

1980

SPRING ARRIVALS

"With Spring's arrival we send our best wishes to you ..."

We were living in Rehoboth Beach, Delaware – one block from the ocean and one block from Lake Gerar. Each spring brought the new baby ducklings with their parents at the lake and sometimes trailing around the yard and down the street.   I'd like to do this design again using beige and yellow for the chicks.

9

1981

SPRINGTIME

"SPRING HAS COME ROUND"
The winter gone,
The spring seems to have just come round;
Hark! With the sweet songs of the birds,
Mountains and fields resound.
Anonymous

This card was made using the photographic method of silk-screening. I drew the pen and ink drawing. I had a friend photographer to reduce the artwork, make a reverse negative which I put on the screen. Using this method you coat the screen with a light sensitive solution and expose the negative positioned on the screen in a box with a light bulb. In a short time the screen is rinsed with water and the stencil is produced directly on the screen.

I seldom used this method, although it is used frequently commercially. The reduction process did not give the clear image that I would have preferred.

1982

CROCUS

"Spring, at last . . ."

We can relate to this sentiment in those winters that seem to last forever. Even the frail yellow and purple crocus poke their heads through the snow. I used the snowflake background to evoke that image.

1983

SPRING PLANTING - . . .

"The snow dissolved, and genial Spring returned
To clothe the fields with verdure. . . ."

Excerpt from "When, to the Attraction of the Busy World"
By William Wordsworth

This one takes a little explaining. With each spring, we watched the Sussex
County farmers till the fields and, lo and behold, the seagulls followed the tractors eating
the bugs unearthed in the process. I was fascinated with this ritual and wanted to portray
this unusual sign of spring. It was very difficult to craft this one so as to be understood
by people all over the country.

1984

FORSYTHIA

"Ah .... Spring!!"

    Okay, I had to try something new again. This time it is the type of paint. I had always used water-based paint. I bought acrylic paints to produce this card. I liked the result, but what a mess on me, equipment, and everywhere. You must use turpentine to remove unwanted paint and I decided to go back to water-based paint after this experience.

1985

SEAGULL II

"Gliding peacefully into the joy of Spring"

I had used the seagull on note cards with the image created by the surrounding paint producing the image. However, Kimber loves seagulls and it seemed time to send a seagull. I used an electric reproducing typewriter for the message for the first time.

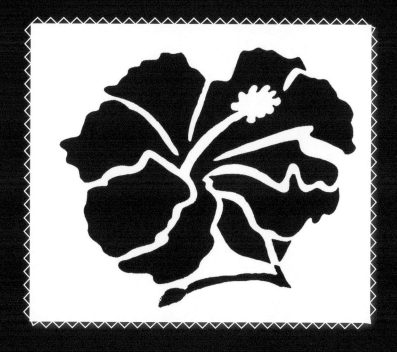

1986

HIBISCUS

"Happy Spring" (The year of the Comet)

Back to hand writing for the message. Also, I added a little gold sticker in the shape of a Comet for this momentous occurrence.

1987

PENELOPE

"We hope you catch the bluebird of Happiness"

    One or two colors just wouldn't work for this card. It is actually a tribute to my cat, Penelope, who had died. Only the Artists Proof shows that, "Penelope 1971 – 1987." Spring cards are to be happy so the message relates that. I won't go into how lovable (unlovable) Penelope actually was during her long life.

1988

IRIS

"Only with winter-patience can we bring
The deep-desired, long-awaited spring."
excerpt from "No Harvest Ripening"
by Anne Morrow Lindbergh

Another experiment —white paint on dark paper.

1989

THE EARLY BIRDIE

"Welcome Spring!"

This was a note card that I really liked. Since we both golf and lots of the spring card recipients also golf, it was a natural. Again, I used the reverse design of having the paint around the white space to form the image.

1990

DAYLILY

"Spring is here!"

I have saved this screen to try different colors in the future. It is a strong design.

1991

TANYA

"Woof! Spring arrived…"

    I wanted to do Tanya not as a memorial, as I had with the cat. Kim tried to help by taking several photos of Tanya with a camellia flower. She got <u>very</u> bored with this as evidenced by the photo here.

1992

HUMMINGBIRD

"It's that time again….
SPRING!!"

This is one of my favorite cards; a simple, yet creative design.

1993

ROOSTER

The "Rooster" is the Chinese symbol for the year 1993. We were both born in years of the "Rooster."

As many of you know, Portugal is a favorite place for us – the "rooster" is the good luck charm of that country.

We are crowing for a good 1993, a Happy Spring, and peace,

From the "Roosters"

1994

OUR HOME IN THE PINES

"Home is where family and friends meet; from our home to your home we send springtime greetings. Happy Spring!"

This card is another example of the photo technique.

1995

BLOSSOM/BUTTERFLY

"Butterflies on wing, birds sing;
Winter is past, Spring at last!"
by Esther S. Dumm

Happy Spring

This card is a tribute to my mother who wrote this poem.

1996

SPRING'S PROMISE

"the promise of Spring"

    Back to the snowflake – A particularly long cold winter brought the snowflake background with the new spring flower sprout card. I was still writing the inside message by hand.

1997

DADDY'S SUNFLOWERS

"Spring, the gateway to Summer,
                    Sunflowers, the faces of Summer"

This card is another two-screen effort remembering the large sunflowers of my childhood and a tribute to my father.

I printed the inside message for the first time on my computer

1998

FLOWER

- A single bloom, so simple, so complete,
A part of spring, always to repeat."

This is the only card that I did not hand silk-screen. As we were moving to Florida, making time for cards was out of the question. I decided to use a small card that Daddy had made and have it reproduced to use as both the Spring card and a change of address

1999

ORANGE BLOSSOMS

"The scent of orange blossoms. Welcome Spring"

What in Florida could welcome Spring? Well, I soon found out. I had never seen or smelled an orange blossom. Wonderful… I added a rubber stamp of a bee to pollinate the blossoms.

2000

HIBISCUS 2

"The Hibiscus, flower of the tropics,
flower of the Treasure Coast."

The 1986 hibiscus in another color.

2001

BOUGOINVILLEA

"Spring – an experience in immortality" (Thoreau)

This card represents the beautiful flowering bush of Florida and is also very much a part of our Portugal experience.

2002

BIRDS OF PARADISE

"Springtime in Florida"

2003

ORCHID

"A clear blue sky,
A welcoming sun appears on the horizon,
While the early buds begin to open,
Ah, a spring day is near."

2004

IRIS 2

"Cherish Yesterday,
Dream Tomorrow,
Live Today."

HAPPY SPRING

This card is a repeat design with lavender paper and purple paint.
It is also one of the few messages that I wrote.

2005

THE ROOSTERS

"ARE YOU A ROOSTER?"

"According to Chinese legend, when the Supreme Being called all the animals to him, 12 came: rat, ox, tiger, hare, dragon, serpent, horse, sheep, monkey, rooster, dog, and pig." Each of these animals was honored with a year and contributed its characteristic traits to that year. It is believed that the year of your birth influences personality, physical and mental attributes, and the success and happiness in your life. The current year is the "Year of the Rooster" and we were both born in "Rooster" years. Rooster people were born in 1921, 1933, 1945, 1957, 1969, 1993, and 2005."

To our family and friends, please join us as we welcome the Spring season.

2006

DAYLILLY 2
"HAPPY SPRINGTIME!!!"

A repeat of the 1990 card in other color paint on white paper.
We made two editions – one in yellow paint and one in orange paint.

Printed in the United States
by Baker & Taylor Publisher Services